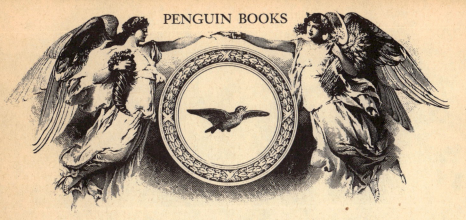

PENGUIN BOOKS

An Exaltation of Larks

The son of a prominent American poet, James Lipton grew up in a literary atmosphere. At twelve he was a published poet; at eighteen, a professional actor who went on to appear in Broadway plays, in films, and on television. He has written Broadway musicals and television dramas, one of which won a "best program" Emmy. In 1976, at the Metropolitan Opera House, he produced one of the most splendid entertainments in New York's history, *The Star Spangled Gala;* and in 1977, at Washington's Kennedy Center, *The New Spirit Inaugural Concert,* which was televised to millions of viewers in the United States and around the world on the occasion of President Carter's inauguration. Of *An Exaltation of Larks,* he says that it "began as a kind of hobby that grew into a passion and finally a book."

An Exaltation of Larks

or,

The Venereal Game

by

James Lipton

PENGUIN BOOKS

For my mother, Betty Lipton,
who showed me the way to words

Penguin Books Ltd, Harmondsworth,
Middlesex, England
Penguin Books, 40 West 23rd Street,
New York, New York 10010, U.S.A.
Penguin Books Australia Ltd, Ringwood,
Victoria, Australia
Penguin Books Canada Limited, 2801 John Street,
Markham, Ontario, Canada L3R 1B4
Penguin Books (N.Z.) Ltd, 182–190 Wairau Road,
Auckland 10, New Zealand

First published in the United States of America by Grossman Publishers 1968
Published in Penguin Books 1977
Reprinted 1977, 1980, 1982, 1983, 1984

LIBRARY OF CONGRESS CATALOGING IN PUBLICATION DATA
Lipton, James.
An exaltation of larks.
Reprint of the 1968 ed. published by Grossman Publishers, New York.
1. English language—Terms and phrases. I. Title.
[PE1689.L5 1977]   427'.09   77-8232
ISBN 0 14 00.4536 8

Printed in the United States of America by
The Murray Printing Company, Westford, Massachusetts
Set in Janson

INTRODUCTION

Most introductions are written in the forlorn expectation that they will be blithely ignored. Not this one. Let me say hastily that this is not an argument for its irresistible allure, either as literature or revelation; but the terrain we will cover has not been widely traveled and I think a glance through this introductory Baedeker will heighten the traveler's enjoyment of his journey.

I strongly suspect that the reader's first reaction, after eagerly opening the cover with its nicely provocative (and I swear not really misleading) subtitle, and arriving not in Gomorrah but Academe, is one of disappointment. This is probably not the anticipated venereal game. Still, I hope that I can appease the disgruntled reader with a titillation nearly as satisfying as the expected one. *This* venereal game is played with language (ours) and words (non-four-letter, that once were ours) and, *caveat lector!*, poetry (that ought to be ours, perhaps). At the outset I hasten to admit that I am not the first explorer in these parts: I see other footprints around me, few and faint, but discernible. Let's begin our journey by following one of these trails. It leads, in a manner of speaking, to Baker Street.

In 1906, having rid himself once and for all of Holmes and Watson, Sir Arthur Conan Doyle returned to the literary form with which he had begun his career fifteen years earlier, producing an historical novel, *Sir Nigel*. In it the young Nigel comes under the tutelage of Sir John Buttesthorn, the Knight of Duplin, head huntsman to the King, and England's greatest authority on the hunt. In Chapter XI, the sublimely immodest old knight says to Nigel: " 'I take shame that you are not more skilled in the mystery of the woods, seeing that I have had the teaching of you, and that no one in broad England is my master at the craft. I pray you to fill your cup again whilst I make use of the little time that is left to us.' "

There follows a lengthy disquisition on the chase, "with many anecdotes, illustrations, warnings and exceptions, drawn from his own great experience" and finally the knight says, " 'But above all I pray you, Nigel, to have a care in the use of the terms of the craft, lest you should make some blunder at table, so that those who are wiser may have the laugh of you, and we who love you may be shamed.'

" 'Nay, Sir John,' said Nigel. 'I think that after your teaching I can hold my place with the others.'

" 'The old knight shook his white head doubtfully. 'There is so much to be learned that there is no one who can be said to know it all,' said he. 'For example, Nigel, it is sooth that for every collection of beasts of the forest, and for every gathering of birds of the air, there is their own private name so that none may be confused with another.'

" 'I know it, fair sir.'

" 'You know it, Nigel, but . . . none can say that they know all, though I have myself pricked off eighty and six for a wager at court, and it is said that the chief huntsman of the Duke of Burgundy has counted over a hundred . . . Answer me now, lad, how would you say if you saw ten badgers together in the forest?'

" 'A cete of badgers, fair sir.'

" 'Good, Nigel—good, by my faith! And if you walk in Woolmer Forest and see a swarm of foxes, how would you call it?'

" 'A skulk of foxes.'

" 'And if they be lions?'

" 'Nay, fair sir, I am not like to meet several lions in Woolmer Forest.'

" 'Ay, lad, but there are other forests besides Woolmer, and other lands besides England, and who can tell how far afield such a knight errant as Nigel of

Tilford may go, when he sees worship to be won? We will say that you were in the deserts of Nubia, and that afterward at the court of the great Sultan you wished to say that you had seen several lions ... How then would you say it?'

" ... 'Surely, fair sir, I would be content to say that I had seen a number of lions, if indeed I could say aught after so wondrous an adventure.'

" 'Nay, Nigel, a huntsman would have said that he had seen a pride of lions, and so proved that he knew the language of the chase. Now, had it been boars instead of lions?'

" 'One says a singular of boars.'

" 'And if they be swine?'

" 'Surely it is a herd of swine.'

" 'Nay, nay, lad, it is indeed sad to see how little you know ... No man of gentle birth would speak of a herd of swine; that is the peasant speech. If you drive them it is a herd. If you hunt them it is other. What call you them then, Edith?'

" 'Nay, I know not.'

" ... 'But you can tell us, Mary?'

" 'Surely, sweet sir, one talks of a sounder of swine.'

"The old Knight laughed exultantly. 'Here is a pupil who never brings me shame! ... Hark ye! only last week that jack-fool, the young Lord of Brocas, was here talking of having seen a covey of pheasants in the wood. One such speech would have been the ruin of a young squire at the court. How would you have said it, Nigel?'

" 'Surely, fair sir, it should be a nye of pheasants.'

" 'Good Nigel—a nye of pheasants, even as it is a gaggle of geese or a badling of ducks, a fall of woodcock or a wisp of snipe. But a covey of pheasants! What sort of talk is that?' "

What sort indeed! This quotation from Conan Doyle makes, for me, the central point about the first two parts of this book: the terms you will discover here are genuine and authentic; that is, each of them, as fanciful—and even frivolous—as some of them may seem, was at one time either in general use as the *only* proper term for a group of whatever beast, fish, fowl or insect it designated,[1] or had acquired sufficient local currency to warrant its inclusion in a list with the well-established hunting terms.

Obviously, at one time or another, every one of these terms had to be invented—and it is equally obvious that much imagination, wit and semantic ingenuity has always gone into that invention: the terms are so charming and poetic it is hard to believe their inventors were unaware of the possibilities open to them, and unconscious of the fun and beauty they were creating. What we have in these terms is clearly the end result of a game that amateur semanticists have been playing for over five hundred years.

Bear in mind that most of these terms were codified in the fifteenth century,[2] a time when the English language was in the process of an expansion—or more accurately, explosion—that can only be compared in importance and scope to the intellectual effusions of Periclean Greece or cinquecento Italy.

The Encyclopaedia Britannica describes as "peculiar to English . . . the extreme receptiveness of its

---

1: Then, as now, as the quotation from Conan Doyle indicates, one would show truly ludicrous ignorance by referring to a herd of fish or a school of elephants.

2: *The Egerton Manuscript,* the earliest surviving list of them, dates from about 1450; *The Book of St. Albans,* the most complete and important of the early lists (and the seminal source for most subsequent compilations), appeared in 1486.

vocabulary to borrowings from other languages." The inhabitants of the island we now call Britain have always shown an astonishing verbal amenability, a quite childlike open-mindedness to and delight in the new. Elizabeth Drew, Chairman of the Department of English at Smith College, has written about the English language, "... no other can communicate such subtle shades of thought and feeling, such fine discriminations of meaning. The riches of its mingled derivations supply a multitude of synonyms ... so that *fatherly* is not the same as *paternal*, nor *fortune* as *luck*, nor *boyish* as *puerile* ..."

I admit to a prejudice toward my own language (and a regrettable inability to read Tolstoi, Dante and the T'ang poets in their original tongues), but I think a good case can be made for English as the preeminent literary language. Compare it to any other; for example, French. Set the starting point of our literary race at the year 1500, the finish-line at 1700. Who shall represent France?—Rabelais, Ronsard, Du Bellay, Jodelle, Montaigne, Malherbe, Corneille, Pascal, Moliere, La Rochefoucauld, Boileau, Racine, La Fontaine, Bossuet, Madame de Sevigne and La Bruyere. This list of two hundred years of French literary genius is generous and comprehensive. Now, let us handicap English by giving French a hundred years' head start; we will set the English starting line at *1600*. In the hundred years that followed it, the English literary genius produced Campion, Donne, Dekker, Beaumont, Lovelace, Jonson, Herrick, Webster, Herbert, Shakespeare, Suckling, Crashaw, Milton, Marvell, Dryden, Bacon, Raleigh, Bunyan, Walton, Pepys, and the forty-seven inspired translators of the King James Bible.[1]

I am well aware that this kind of contest is in a sense invidious; how do you compare one writer's

---

1: Excluded from the list as a further handicap are such giants as Pope, Defoe and Swift whose *major* works appeared after 1700.

genius with another's, Moliere's, for example, with Shake-speare's, or Dante's with Cervantes'? The answer, of course, is that you don't and shouldn't. But the oeuvre of two different periods, or two nations, *can* be compared, and on this basis I think that the literary production of any nation, ranged alongside English, may find itself shadowed. And, finally, I think that this eminence of English as a literary language can best be explained by the unique flexibility and omnivorous word-hunger of the generations of Britons who forged the uncommonly keen sword wielded by our belletristic heroes.

An accident of geography played a large part in the process. The British Isle, lying fat and fecund behind a low, beckoning coastline and narrow, unforbidding moat, was an irresistible lure to the peoples of the mainland. The historian G. M. Trevelyan, in his *History of England*, a book as admirable for its exquisite literary style as for its historiology, says, "The temptation to invade the island lay not only in the pearls, the gold and the tin for which it seems to have been noted . . . long before the foundation of Rome; temptation lay also in its fertile soil, the rich carpet of perennial green that covered the downs and every clearing in the forest, the absence of long interludes of frost that must have seemed miraculous in a land so far to the North before men knew the secret of the Gulf Stream."

And with each new wave of traders or invaders came new semantic blood, new ideas and new ways of expressing them. The narrow, languid brook of the Celtic tongue suddenly acquired a powerful tributary as the splendid geometry of the Latin language burst into it, bringing such lofty sounds and concepts as *intellect, fortune, philosophy, education, victory, gratitude.* From 449 on, the blunt, intensely expressive monosyllables of the Anglo-Saxons joined the swelling stream, giving us the names of the strong, central elements of our lives: *God, earth, sun, sea, win, lose, live, love* and *die*. Then, in the eleventh century, with the Norman Conquest, a great warm gush of French sonorities—*emotion, pity, peace, devotion, romance*—swelled the torrent to a flood-tide that burst its banks, spreading out in broad, loamy deltas black with the rich silt of WORDS.

It was in precisely this word-hungry, language-mad England that the terms you will encounter in this book were born. They are prime examples both of the infinite subtlety of our language and the wild imagination and verbal skill of our forebears. The terms were codified during the period when the river of words was approaching its greatest breadth, beginning in about 1450 with *The Egerton Manuscript*.

These terms and phrases, like the other verbal inventions of their time, were not idly made, but were intended for, and in many cases achieved, wide currency and acceptance. As you will see in Part I of this book, a number of them have come down to this day, and are accepted, taken-for-granted figures of speech. What is most remarkable to me about this rich repository of poetry is that all the terms in it can be said to be correct, proper, and usable. The lyrical, fanciful EXALTATION OF LARKS has credentials as good as the mundane and universally accepted SCHOOL OF FISH, since both terms offer as provenance the same source, the list in *The Book of St. Albans*. The fact is that AN EXALTATION OF LARKS is the 18th term in the list and A SCHOOL OF FISH is the 132nd. Such whimsies as A SHREWDNESS OF APES and A COWARDICE OF CURS also precede the more familiar fish term (109th and 117th).[1]

So, one can certainly argue with good logic that *every* one of the terms you will find in the first

---

1: There are a number of expressions in our contemporary speech that have the form of these terms and obviously derive from the order. We will let one stand for them all: a chorus of complaint.

8   two parts of this book has an equal claim on our respect and loyalty. The fact that many of them have slipped out of our common speech can only, I think, be described as lamentable. There is little enough poetry in our speech (and lives) to continue to ignore a vein as rich as this. The purpose of this book is to try, in an admittedly modest measure, to redress the balance. The thesis of this book can be summed up very simply: when a group of ravens flaps by, you should, if you want to refer to their presence, say, "There goes an unkindness of ravens." Anything else would be wrong.

     The reader may have noticed that, until this moment, I have avoided giving a single, comprehensive collective term to these collective terms. That is because there isn't any. Oddly enough, the compilers of the numerous lists of these words, though obviously enthusiastic philologists, have never felt compelled to settle on a group term for them. The explorer in this field will find these words variously referred to as "nouns of multitude," "company terms," "nouns of assemblage," "collective nouns,"[1] "group terms," and "terms of venery." This last seems to me best and most appropriate, and itself warrants some explanation.

     "Venery" and its adjective, "venereal," are most often thought of, of course, as signifying love, and more specifically physical love. From *Venus* we have the Latin root *ven* which appears in the word *venari*, meaning "to hunt game." Eric Partridge, in his etymological dictionary *Origins*, asserts that the *ven* in *venari* has its original meaning: "to desire (and therefore) to pursue," and he sees a close connection between it and the word "win," from the Middle English *winnen*, and even the Sanskrit *vanoti*, "he conquers." It is in this sense that venery

---

1: I hold this to be a misnomer since, obviously, it can be confused with the strictly grammatical term referring to such words as "majority." The same may be said of "nouns of multitude."

came to signify the hunt, and it was so used in all the early works on the chase, including the earliest known on the subject of English hunting, *Le Art* [sic] *de Venery*, written in Norman French in the 1320's by the huntsman of Edward II, Master William Twici.

So, if all the earlier and far greater experts in this field have left it to someone of the twentieth century to select the proper term for these proper terms, I (cautiously and with boundless and well-founded humility) pick up the gauntlet and declare for "terms of venery"; if for no more cogent reason than that it allows of such disingenuous derivative delights as "venereal," "venerealize," and "venerealization" (*vide* Part III of this book).

So be it. Henceforward we are talking about terms of venery or venereal terms.

Before beginning the list of the authentic venereal terms themselves, a word is in order on the various *types* of terms. Etymologically speaking, the order of venereal terms seems to me to break down into six families, according to the apparent original inspiration for the term. I would list the six families as:

1: *Onomatopoeia:* for example, A MURMURATION OF STARLINGS, A GAGGLE OF GEESE.
2: *Characteristic:* A LEAP OF LEOPARDS, A SKULK OF FOXES. This is by far the largest family.
3: *Appearance:* A KNOT OF TOADS, A BOUQUET OF PHEASANTS.
4: *Habitat:* A SHOAL OF BASS, A NEST OF RABBITS.
5: *Comment* (pro or con, reflecting the observer's point of view): A RICHNESS OF MARTENS, A COWARDICE OF CURS.
6: *Error* (resulting from an incorrect transcription by a scribe or printer, faithfully preserved in the corrupted form by subsequent compilers): A SCHOOL OF FISH, originally "shoal."

The preceding six families of venereal terms are my invention. In the lists that follow I will not indicate to which family I would assign each term, preferring to leave it to the reader to decide whether A MURDER OF CROWS belongs in the second or fifth family. These decisions are proper moves in the venereal game.

All of the authentic terms you are about to encounter received their first official stamp in the so-called Books of Courtesy, medieval and fifteenth-century social primers, intended, as the quotation from *Sir Nigel* indicates, to provide a gentleman with the means of social acceptability, and to spare him the embarrassment of "some blunder at table, so that those who are wiser may have the laugh of you, and we who love you may be shamed."[1] The Books dealt with a variety of subjects, but in the largely rural England of that time, the section on the Hunt was doubtless the most important. And in nearly all the Books of Courtesy, the authors saw fit to transcribe a list of the proper, accepted terms of venery. After *Egerton* (the earliest surviving manuscript, referred to earlier in a footnote), most of the lists were based on previous compilations, always with some omissions, errors and additions. In spite of this variance, each succeeding list gave greater weight of authority to the terms. In the fifteenth century there were several important manuscripts containing lists of terms. In addition to the *Egerton*, which contained one hundred six terms in its list, there were two *Harley Manuscripts*, with forty-eight terms in the first and forty-five in the second, *The Porkington Manuscript*, with one hundred nine, *The Digby* and *The Robert of Gloucester Manuscripts*, each with fifty.

1: William Blades, in his Introduction to the 1881 facsimile edition of *The Book of St. Albans*, refers to the book's subjects as "those with which, at that period, every man claiming to be 'gentle' was expected to be familiar; while ignorance of their laws and language was to confess himself a 'churl.'"

The subject was of such importance
that, in about 1476, within a year of the establishment of
printing in England, a printed book, *The Hors, Shepe, &
the Ghoos*, appeared, with a list of one hundred six venereal
terms. But by far the most important of the early works
on the subject was *The Book of St. Albans*, with its list of
one hundred sixty-four terms, printed in 1486 at St. Albans
by "the schoolmaster printer."

The accredited author was, interest-
ingly, a woman, Dame Juliana Barnes, reputedly the sister
of Lord Berners and prioress of the nunnery of Sopewell.
There has, however, been considerable debate on the subject of Dame Juliana, with some authorities insisting she
was a pure invention and others arguing strenuously for
her existence. William Blades, a great expert on early English printing, came out staunchly for Dame Juliana in his
Introduction to the facsimile edition of *The Book of St.
Albans*. In it he inveighs against most of her biographers
for only adding to the mystery with their highly imaginative accounts of her life. At one point an "expert" read
her name as Julyan and produced a learned biography of
a man. So she remained, writes Blades, until "Chauncy,
in 1700 (History of Hertfordshire) restored her sex . . .
and then set to work upon making a family for her. His
first discovery was that, being a 'Dame,' she was of noble
blood. Finding also that the family name of Lord Berners
was, in olden time, spelt occasionally Barnes, he soon sup-
plied a father for our authoress, in the person of Sir James
Berners. And so the game of making history went on mer-
rily. . . . But enough of such sham biography; let us return
to facts. The word 'Dame' did not in the fifteenth century
. . . imply any connection with a titled family, it meant
simply Mistress or Mrs. . . . Allowing that Lord Berners'
name was sometimes spelt Barnes, is that sufficient reason
for making our authoress a member of his family? I think
not."

Having disposed of falsehood, Blades argues for the truth of Dame Juliana's existence, largely from internal evidence in the Book itself, finally committing himself to the extent of pronouncing her "England's earliest poetess." He allows for the possibility that two parts of the Book, on Hawking and Heraldry, may be the work of the anonymous "schoolmaster printer," but he grants Dame Juliana undisputed authorship of the part on Hunting (the one with which we are concerned).

Other authorities have held that the entire *Book of St. Albans* is nothing but a compilation of earlier works and folk material, put together by one or several printers under the collective *nom de plume* of Dame Juliana. At this distance we cannot decide the matter, and so it seems that Dame Juliana is doomed to suffer the literary fate of Homer (there could be worse). Whether Homer was one blind poet or several generations of nameless bards, and whether Dame Juliana was a lone and quite extraordinary prioress or A PLAGIARY OF PRINTERS in the fifteenth century, the important fact remains that *The Book of St. Albans* is the definitive work on the subject at hand, and a fascinating work by any standard.[1]

It contains three parts, the first on Hawking, the second on Hunting, and the third on Heraldry. The book on Hawking contains such paragraph headings as "A medecyne for an hawke that has loft here courage."[2] and "The maner how a man fhall put an hawke in to mewe—and that is to be wele nooted."

The first book ends by assigning certain hawks to certain ranks, thus: "Theys hawkes belong to an

---

1: In 1496, the famous and aptly named Wynken de Worde (the aptness is no coincidence: his real name was Jan van Wynken), successor to the first English printer, William Caxton, reprinted *The Book of St. Albans*, and in the sixteenth century there were more than a dozen new editions of the book.

2: In this section I have retained the language of the Book, with its long s's and its "ys" and "is" plurals, to give some of the flavor of the original. I don't think translation is necessary; the contemporary eye adjusts quickly to the dusk of fifteenth century orthography.

Emproure . . . Theis hawkes belong to a kyng . . . For a prince . . . For a duke . . . For an erle . . . for a Baron . . . Hawkes for a knyght . . . Hawkis for a Squyer[1] . . . For a lady[2] . . . An hawke for a young man," and the section concludes with "And yit ther be moo kyndis of hawkes," listing them, then closes with "*Explicit*."[3]

The second book, the one that concerns us, on Hunting, begins with a brief foreword by Dame Juliana: "Lyke Wiſe as i the booke of hawkyng aforeſayd . . ." "Likewise, as in the book of hawking aforesaid are written and noted the terms of pleasure belonging to gentlemen having delight therein, in the same manner this book following showeth to such gentle persons the manner of hunting for all manner of beasts, whether they be beasts of venery, or of chase, or Rascal.[4] And also it showeth all the terms convenient as well to the hounds as to the beasts aforesaid. And in certain there be many diverse of them as it is declared in the book following."

There follow two septets, a form popularized a hundred years earlier by Chaucer, each comprising three rhymed couplets and an internally rhymed con-

---

1: These variant spellings, Theys and Theis, Hawkes and Hawkis, sometimes occurring in the same line of text, are common in early English printing.

2: Each of these headings is followed by a list of the proper hawks, *e.g.*, "Ther is a Merlyon. And that hawke is for a lady."

3: An abbreviation of *explicitus est liber*, "the book is unfolded" (from the time when it was in fact a rolled parchment). It usually appears in colophons with the author's name, and is simply a fifteenth-century way of signifying The End.

4: The four beasts of venery were the red deer (hart and hind), hare, boar and wolf. The four beasts of the chase were the fallow deer (buck and doe), fox, marten and roe. C. E. Hare, in *The Language of Field Sports*, writes that "rascal" originally meant "rabble" or "mob," and that it was a hunting term "applied to all beasts other than the four beasts of venery, and the four beasts of the chase." All three groups were locked in a rigid hierarchic order. Conan Doyle's Knight of Duplin is firm on the subject: "He also spoke of the several ranks and grades of the chase: how the hare, hart, and boar must ever take precedence over the buck, the doe, the fox, the marten and the roe, even as a knight banneret does over a knight, while these in turn are of a higher class to the badger, the wildcat, or the otter, who are but the common populace of the world of beasts."

cluding line. The first septet is called "Beſtýs of venerý," the second "Beſtýs of the Chace."

The entire book is addressed to "My dere chylde" (in the second line of the opening poem). Further on in the text we encounter such phrases as "Do so, my child," "Think what I say, my son," etc. This maternal tone in the book is one of the most frequently advanced arguments for Dame Juliana's authorship.

The book continues almost entirely in verse, with such titles as "What is a bevý of Roos grete or ſmall" and "The rewarde for howndýs." It contains a very long poem called "How ýe ſhall breeche an hert," with explicit instructions for removing "the finale gutties . . . the leuer [liver] . . . and after that the bledder . . ." and concludes on the recto of sig. tiiij (the 24th page) with "Explicit Dam Julyans Barnes in her boke of huntyng." Though this would seem to end the book, in fact, and to our eternal good fortune, it does not. Because of Dame Juliana's colophon here there has been some argument as to the authorship of the seven pages following it which conclude the book of Hunting and contain, among other things, the famous venereal list. This is one of the principal reasons that the schoolmaster printer sometimes shares creative credit with the prioress.

Whatever their authorship, the seven pages contain treatises in both poetry and prose on such subjects as "The propreteis of a goode Grehound" and "The propretees [sic, another example of variant spelling] of a goode hors," followed by a battery of maxims and homilies under the heading "Merke wele theýs iiii thýnges." One of the things to be marked well is:

Too Wyues in oon hous [Two wives in one house], too cattys and oon mous.

Too dogges and oon boon: Theis ſhall neu accord I oon.

And then, on the facing recto page, we find the title "The Compaýnýs of beeſtýs and fowlýs," followed by two vertical columns beginning with "An Herde of Hertis" (harts), and continuing, in fifteenth-century English, through an exhaustive list of one hundred sixty-four venereal terms, some surprising, some amusing, and some arrestingly beautiful. The most startling thing about the list is that not all of the terms in it refer to beeſtys and fowlys. Of Dame Juliana's (or the schoolmaster printer's) quite astonishing digressions into the realm of poetry and wit, more will be said in Part III of this book. For now, we will confine ourselves to the true and authentic terms of the hunt, compiled not only from *The Book of St. Albans* but from all the available manuscripts and books on the subject.

The list of venereal terms in this book is intended neither as etymology nor zoology. None of these musings pretend to a high order of scholarship. They are at most an innocent summer ramble through unfamiliar fields; any discoveries made along the way are fortuitous and no enlightenment is promised. In fact, the one tree we will probably *not* encounter is the bodhi. The venereal list that follows is not complete, comprehensive or final. If it is anything more than meets the eye, perhaps it is literary, in the sense that T. S. Eliot once described literature as "the impulse to transcribe one's thoughts correctly." Our language, one of our most precious natural resources in the English-speaking countries, is also a dwindling one that deserves at least as much protection as our woodlands, streams and whooping cranes. We don't write letters, we make long-distance calls; we don't read, we are talked to, in the resolutely twelve-year-old vocabulary of radio and television. Under the banner of Timesaving we are offered only the abbreviated, the abridged, the aborted. Our Noble Eightfold Path consists entirely of shortcuts. And what are we urged to do with the time saved by these means? Skim through the *Reader's Digest* at eighteen hundred words a minute, eating a pre-cooked dinner of condensed soup and reconstituted meat and vegetables on a jet going six hundred miles an hour. Refreshed by our leisurely holiday we can then plunge back into the caucus-race with renewed vigor, dashing breathless behind the Dodo toward an ever-re-treating finish-line. Before it is too late I would like to pro-pose a language sanctuary, a wild-word refuge, removed and safe from the hostile environment of our TV-tabloid world.

Perhaps it is already too late. Under the influence of film and television especially (both valuable but intensely pictorial arts) the picture is finally *replacing* those maligned thousand words. Soon, if all goes badly, we may be reduced to a basic vocabulary of a few hundred smooth, homogenized syllables, and carry tiny movie pro-jectors and bandoliers of miniaturized film cartridges to project our more important thoughts (too precious to entrust to mere words) in the proper pictorial form on our shirtfront for our conversational partner. Eventually we may be able to press a button on our belt and produce an instantaneous, abstract, psychedelic, atonal, aleatory light-show that will penetrate straight to the beholder's chromo-somes, influencing not only him or her, but logophobic generations yet unborn. Wordless, we will build the new Jerusalem!

But, for now, while we are still en-meshed in the encumbering toils of language, perhaps this list of terms will slightly expand our means of performing the most difficult feat on earth: transferring one thought from one mind to another. I assume this is an important task, or why else would Eliot be concerned about tran-scribing his "thoughts correctly," or Dylan Thomas have written, "I hack/This rumpus of shapes[1]/For you to know/ How I, a spinning man,/ Glory also this star . . ."? Wordsworth, in the famous *Preface to the Second Edition of Lyrical Ballads* in which he formulated the often quoted definition of poetry as "emotion recollected in tranquility," even had the audacity to describe the poet as "a man speaking to men." Coleridge muttered stubbornly that poetry was "the best words in their best order," and even the angels are on our side (or vice versa), for we find "How forcible are right words" in Job 6:25, and "A word fitly spoken is like apples of gold in pictures of silver" in Proverbs 25:11. Hart Crane, in an excess of philologic zeal that would have earned him the contempt of some of our contemporary theorists, dared to exclaim, "One must be drenched in words, literally soaked in them, to have the right ones form themselves into the proper patterns at the right moment," and in one of the *Four Quartets* Eliot admits that "Our concern was speech, and speech impelled us/To purify the language of the tribe." High contemporary marks to Mr. Eliot for the tribal reference, but F for preferring speech to macaronic chants and mind-blowing mumbo-jumbo. [2]

It may be argued that our language has in fact grown in the past quarter of a century, at least in two areas: science and slang. Certainly the language of the laboratory and the launching pad has begun to seep into our common speech, and some of the words and phrases we are using freely now have an awesome, transcendental beauty: *supersonic, module, cyclotron, transistor, helix,*

1: Note, in passing, the venereal term. They are not uncommon in Dylan's work. Witness A COVEN OF KETTLES in *Under Milk Wood*, and A SPRINGUL OF LARKS in *Poem in October*.

2: A genuine F, perhaps, for "borrowing" *Donner un sens plus pur aux mots de la tribu*, without acknowledging its author, Mallarmé.

retrorocket, isotope, stereo . . . even *ballistic missile*, which, in spite of its ominous significance, has a stunning echoic sound. The majority of the scientific words, however, are still Greek and Latin monstrosities with all the charm and euphony of *eccentroösteochondrodysplasia.*

For a short while it looked as though American slang might enrich the language, particularly the sinuous patois of the black American and his mimics, denizens of the rock and jazz worlds, the young, the hip, and the would-be hip. New uses for old words like *cool, dig* and *rip off* were pungent, useful additions to our speech. There was evidence of originality and imagination in small poetic flights like *mind-blowing, turn on, uptight* and *hangup* (the latter two of which seem much more expressive than *anxious* or *neurosis*). Being a folk art, popular music reflects the public mind, and the songs of the generation that grew up in the Sixties have shown some ingenuity and daring in both themes and words. The best lyrics of Bob Dylan, Paul Simon and Joni Mitchell are closer in style to Rimbaud's symbolism than Tin Pan Alley's sentimentalism.

The drawback is that the "revolution" has virtually buried itself in a numbing welter of repetition. *Right on* and *out of sight* begin to lose their charm on the ten-thousandth hearing, and the *far out* family of superlatives, by elbowing aside nearly every other adjective in a generation's speech, doesn't expand the language, it diminishes it.

Words, said T. S. Eliot, "slip, slide, perish/ Decay with imprecision, will not stay in place,/ Will not stay still," and Elizabeth Drew (quoted earlier) has written, "Language is like soil. However rich, it is subject to erosion, and its fertility is constantly threatened by uses that exhaust its vitality. It needs constant re-invigoration if it is not to become arid and sterile. Poetry is one great source of the maintenance and renewal of language."

And the poetry need not come exclusively from poets. In fact, the poet and critic Louis Untermeyer has written, "We cannot escape from poetry. We need its power of quick communication in every casual activity . . . The very man who belittles poetry in public practices it in private . . . His dreams are poetry . . . his simples sentences rely on the power of imagery . . . we delight to intensify a hard drizzle by saying 'it's raining cats and dogs.' . . . [A] good servant is not merely rare but 'scarce as hen's teeth,' . . . The fruit-grower . . . capitalizes the power of poetry by saying that [his oranges] are *Sunkist*, a conceit worthy of the Elizabethan singers . . . The architect daringly suggests the tower of Babel with the 'skyscraper'; the man in the street intensifies his speech by tightening it into slang, the shorthand of the people, by 'crashing' a party, 'muscling' in, 'hitting' the high spots. Language is continually being made swift and powerful through the medium of the poetic phrase."

So, here are some new candidates for our contemporary lexicon. They are the trophies of what has been, for me, a long and exciting search that began when I realized with a sudden exhilarating shiver that GAGGLE OF GEESE and PRIDE OF LIONS might not be just isolated pools of amusing poetic idiosyncrasy but estuaries leading to a virtually uncharted sea, sparkling with found poetry—and intriguing poetic possibilities. Every curious soul has its moment on that peak in Darien. That was mine and it led to these pages.

I have two hopes: one, that the evangelistic tone of this preface will be forgiven, and, two, that a few of these terms, from Parts I and II—and even from Part III—will stick to our ribs and be ingested into our speech. If they do, it isn't just that we will be able to turn to someone and coolly and correctly say, "Look— a charm of finches." What is more important is that a charm of poetry will have quietly slipped into our lives.

PART I

THE KNOWN

This brief list contains the genuine terms of venery that are still a part of our living speech. They are as old as the other terms that follow, but we still use them, and it is this fact that has led me to separate them from their brothers. They may be so familiar to our ear that we say or read them without thinking; they have lost their poetry for us.

But stand back for a moment from some of these familiar terms—A PLAGUE OF LOCUSTS, A BROOD OF HENS, A LITTER OF PUPS (plague! brood! *litter!*)—and perhaps their aptness and daring will reappear.

So with all the terms in this part: we begin on familiar ground, to sharpen our senses by restoring the magic to the mundane.

A SCHOOL OF FISH

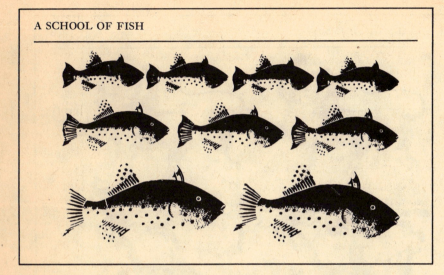

As noted earlier, school *was a corruption of* shoal, *a term still in use for specific fish* (vide Part II). *C. E. Hare, in* The Language of Field Sports, *quotes John Hodgkin on this term arguing that* school *and* shoal *are in fact variant spellings of the same word, but Eric Partridge, I think correctly, sees them coming from two different roots, the former from ME* scole, *deriving from the Latin* schola, *a school, and the latter from the OE* sceald, *meaning shallow. I think it is obvious that in the lexicon of venery* shoal *was meant and* school *is a corruption.*

A PRIDE OF LIONS

A HERD OF ELEPHANTS

A LITTER OF PUPS

A FLOCK OF SHEEP

A BAND OF MEN

Hence also band *for a group of musicians.*

A SLATE OF CANDIDATES

Doubtless deriving from the time when nominees' names were chalked on one.

A SWARM OF BEES

A BROOD OF HENS

An interesting term this. J. Donald Adams, in The Magic and Mystery of Words, *says, "Angels in any quantity may be referred to only as a* host. *The word's title to that distinction is clear enough;* host *derives from the Latin* hostis, *meaning enemy, and hence came to mean an army. It was presumably applied to angels as the warriors of God."*

A BEVY OF BEAUTIES

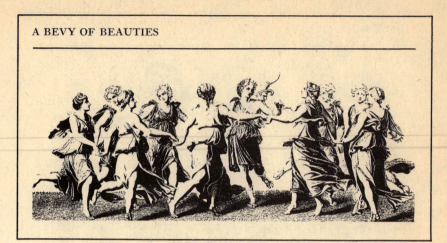

This is one of the few venereal terms whose origin is uncertain. Partridge marks it o.o.o.—of obscure origin; but hazards the guess that it derives from the Old French bevee, *a drink or drinking.*

A STRING OF PONIES

A COVEY OF PARTRIDGES

Here is an interesting etymological journey: the Latin cubare *means "to be lying down" (both* concubine, *to be lying down* with, *and* incubate, *to be lying down* on, *also derive from this root). It becomes* cover *in Old French, whence* cove *or* covy *in Middle English. Thus it refers to nesting habits.*

A PLAGUE OF LOCUSTS

A COLONY OF ANTS

A PASSEL OF BRATS

An American term, of course. J. Donald Adams went looking for this one, finding it finally in Wentworth's American Dialect Dictionary as "hull passel of young ones," "a passel o' hogs," etc., but no etymology is given. My Southern friends assure me, however, that passel *is simply "parcel" in a regional accent.*

PART II

THE UNKNOWN

These terms are authentic and authoritative. They were used, they were correct, and they are useful, correct—and available—today.

A MURDER OF CROWS

A KINDLE OF KITTENS

Kin, kindred, *and the German* Kinder *are related to this word from the ME* kindlen. *To* kindle *literally means "to give birth."*

A COWARDICE OF CURS

A LEAP OF LEOPARDS

The derivation of this word is obvious, since a pod *contains several peas. It was borrowed by sailors to describe groups of seals.*

A SLOTH OF BEARS

A RAFTER OF TURKEYS

Probably not what you think, if you see birds sitting on a beam. The term is related to raft *in the sense of "a large and often motley collection of people and things, as a* raft *of books," according to Webster. It is also related to* raff, *which means a collection of things, and appears in some interesting variations in* riffraff *and* raffish. *Remember* raff, *we will encounter it again.*

A PACE OF ASSES

From the Latin passus, *a step or stride.*

A WALK OF SNIPE

A GAM OF WHALES

A whaling voyage could last as long as three years, so when two whalers encountered each other on some remote sea, it called for a gam, an exchange of crews via whaleboats and the "gamming chair." It was a happy time for a whaleman and, obviously, the whales' habit of sporting playfully on the surface of the sea gave rise to this fanciful term.

A NEST OF RABBITS

A GANG OF ELK

A FALL OF WOODCOCKS

A DULE OF DOVES

A corruption of the French deuil, *mourning. The soft, sad ululation of the dove has always evoked an association with mourning.*

A WEDGE OF SWANS

Since the publication of the first edition of this book, many correspondents have inquired about the omission of a term for swans. The splendid sight of a group of swans, they reason, cannot have escaped the notice of the Knight of Duplin and his eager coevals. My correspondents are partially correct. There is indeed a term for swans, but its inclusion here should put to rest any questions about its omission in earlier editions: it is a singularly colorless term for so inviting a subject. But we can take heart from Eliot's assertion, quoted earlier, that words "slip, slide . . . will not stay in place," which is simply to say that the swans—and the English language—await your creative contribution.

As do, perhaps, the next five terms, which, like the wedge of swans, arrived at the gangplank after the first edition of this book had sailed. Here they are, for better or worse, for the first time, for your critical and by now informed judgment.

A PARTY OF JAYS

A COMPANY OF PARROTS

A COLONY OF PENGUINS

A COVER OF COOTS

See the previous note on partridges.

A SORD OF MALLARDS

In Old French sordre *meant to rise up in flight.*

A SKULK OF FOXES

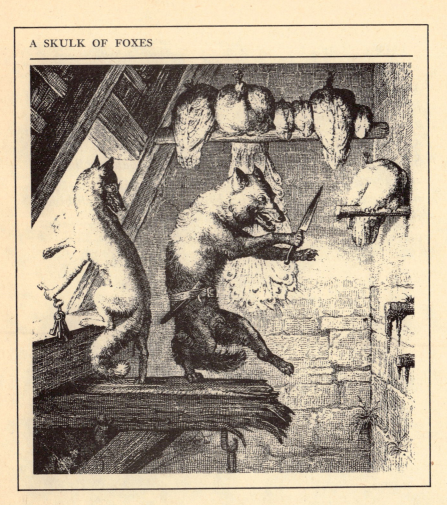

38 A DISSIMULATION OF BIRDS

A PEEP OF CHICKENS

A BUSINESS OF FERRETS

A PITYING OF TURTLEDOVES

A PADDLING OF DUCKS
on water.

A BEVY OF ROEBUCKS

See earlier note on BEVY OF BEAUTIES. *When applied to roes there would seem to be some support for the argument that it stems from the French word for drinking, since roes would frequently be seen together at a watering place.*

A CRASH OF RHINOCEROSES

A SIEGE OF HERONS

From the way the heron doggedly waits for its prey in the shallows at its feet.

To my knowledge no one has ever successfully tracked this term to its lair. C. E. Hare suspects that it may be one of the erroneous terms, a corruption of dule, *since early scribes sometimes confused turtledoves with turtles.*

A HOVER OF TROUT

A HUSK OF HARES

Vide *the note on* BALE OF TURTLES. *This is probably also a member of the sixth family of venereal terms, an error which became the rule.*

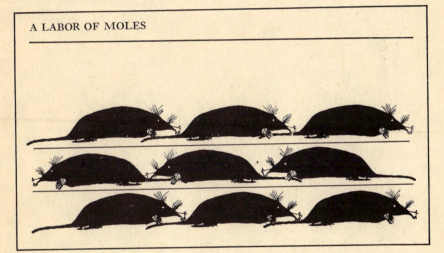

A LABOR OF MOLES

A RAG OF COLTS

There has been considerable conjecture about this term. It may be related to rage, *a word we will encounter later in another context; it may derive from the Old Norse* rögg *(whence "rug"), signifying something shaggy (like a colt's coat). Hare conjectures that it is the word that became our word "rack," one of the gaits of a five-gaited horse.*

A DRIFT OF HOGS

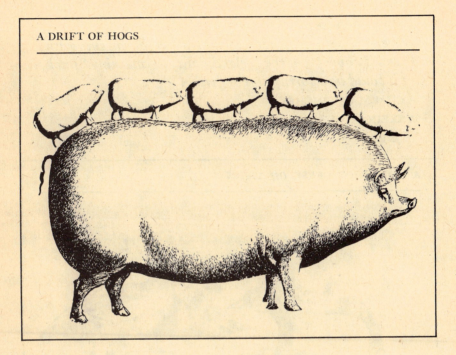

A TRIP OF GOATS
A very widely used term, given by eighteen authorities.
It could come from the Icelandic thrypa, *meaning "flock,"*
or it could be a corruption of "tribe."

A CHARM OF FINCHES

A SKEIN OF GEESE
in flight.

A GAGGLE OF GEESE *on water*

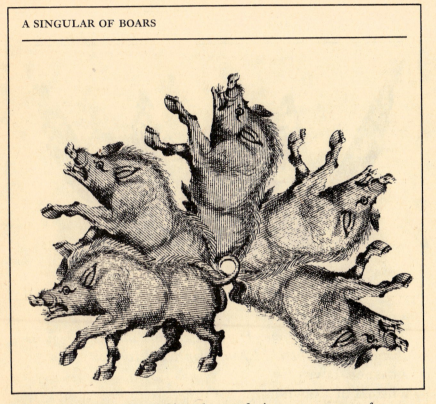

What have we here? Singular *to designate a group of any-thing?* Singular *is obviously an English scribe's translitera-tion of* sanglier, *the French word for "boar," which was, in its turn, a French transliteration of "boar" in Latin,* singu-laris porcus. *Now,* singularis porcus *certainly seems to imply that the boar travels alone, hence needs, and deserves, no group term—until one recalls that in Latin, as in English, the word "singular" means both "solitary" and "extraordi-nary," whereas the exclusive sense of "solitary" or "single" was usually consigned to* singulus. *A "single" look at the illustration on this page unravels the riddle.* Singularis, sanglier *and* singular *all mean "extraordinary."*

A TIDINGS OF MAGPIES

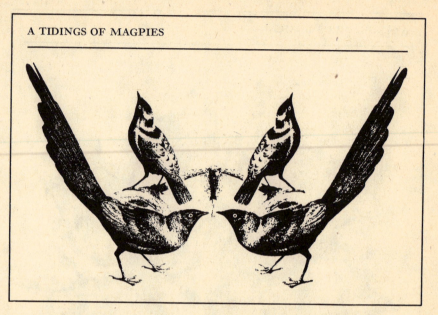

A CETE OF BADGERS
Another obscure one. Hare makes the interesting guess that it may be the old Chaucerian word for "city."

A CAST OF HAWKS

A DECEIT OF LAPWINGS

AN OSTENTATION OF PEACOCKS

A DROVE OF CATTLE

A BOUQUET OF PHEASANTS

48   A CONGREGATION OF PLOVERS
A TROOP OF KANGAROOS
AN UNKINDNESS OF RAVENS
A BUILDING OF ROOKS
From their nesting habits.
A RICHNESS OF MARTENS
A HOST OF SPARROWS
See the previous note on angels.

A SOUNDER OF SWINE

This is one of those words that suffered some interesting sea-changes hopping back and forth across the English Channel. Originally it was the Old English word sunor, *meaning herd. The Norman French adopted it and it became Gallicized to* soundre. *Since Norman French was the language of all the earliest hunting treatises, and thus the principal source of hunting terms, the word returned to England as* sounder, *with the English none the wiser that they were borrowing back their own rake. The hunting word "redingote" made a similar trip. The snobbish French affected the English word "riding-coat" which, in their accent, became re-din-goat. The snobbish English, affecting French, heard the word, thought it French, and took it back across the Channel as redingote, which it has remained to this day.*

A CLUTCH OF EGGS

A DRAY OF SQUIRRELS
A Middle English word for their nests.

AN ARMY OF CATERPILLARS

A FLIGHT OF SWALLOWS

A CRY OF PLAYERS
The proper venereal term for a troupe of actors in the sixteenth century.

A CLOWDER OF CATS

A truly marvelous venereal term that somehow conveys the essence of cats in a group. Hodgkin, in Proper Terms, *says that it is probably the same word as "clutter."*

A WATCH OF NIGHTINGALES

A BARREN OF MULES

The term seems to refer to their sterility, but Hodgkin suspects that barren *(or, as it appears in most of the lists,* baren) *was a corruption of the ME* berynge, *"bearing," and, in the same sense,* The Egerton Manuscript *has "a Burdynne of Mulysse."*

A SHREWDNESS OF APES

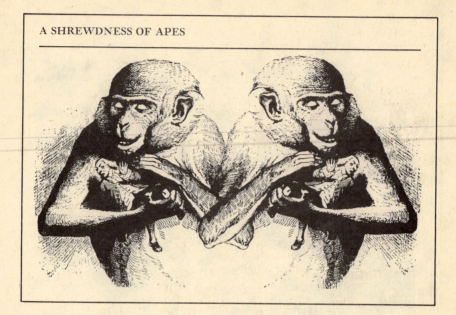

A ROUTE OF WOLVES

In Old French route *meant a troop or throng.*

56   A MURMURATION OF STARLINGS
      A SPRING OF TEAL
      A SMACK OF JELLYFISH
      A HARRAS OF HORSES
      Hara *in Latin meant a pigsty, hence any enclosure for animals.*
      A PENCIL OF LINES
      A proper contemporary group term in mathematics.

A PARLIAMENT OF OWLS

PART III

THE UNEXPECTED

In the Introduction to this book I mentioned "the astonishing digressions into the realm of pure poetry and wit" of Dame Juliana, or the schoolmaster printer, or *whoever* wrote *The Book of St. Albans*. As I said, there were one hundred sixty-four terms of venery in that book. You have now read many of them (with the terms from various other sources) in the preceding pages. It will probably surprise you, as it did me, to discover that of the one hundred sixty-four venereal terms in *The Book of St. Albans, seventy* of them refer not to animals but to people and life in the fifteenth century and every one of these social venereal terms makes the same kind of affectionate or mordant comment that the strictly field terms do.

               By 1486 venereal terms were already a game, capable of codification; and if you think that the social terms were casually intended and soon forgotten, be advised that the second such term in the *St. Albans* list (it is the ninth term in actual order) is the still very much alive A BEVY OF LADIES; and the seventeenth term on the list is none other than A CONGREGATION OF PEOPLE, a true venereal term, coming between A WALK OF SNIPES and AN EXALTATION OF LARKS.

               The social terms are scattered throughout the list, with nothing to distinguish them from the hunting terms. Obviously the compiler considered *all* the terms equally valid and important to anyone anxious to avoid the title of "churl." The social terms are so surprising, and marked with such witty revelation, that I would be remiss not to include a number of them in this book. Herewith, some highlights from the venereal game, as it was played in *The Book of St. Albans* in the year of our Lord 1486.

A HERD OF HARLOTS

A SUPERFLUITY OF NUNS

Henry VIII was as yet unborn, but the ground was obviously fertile for his quarrel with Rome.

A SCHOOL OF CLERKS

A CONVERTING OF PREACHERS

A DOCTRINE OF DOCTORS

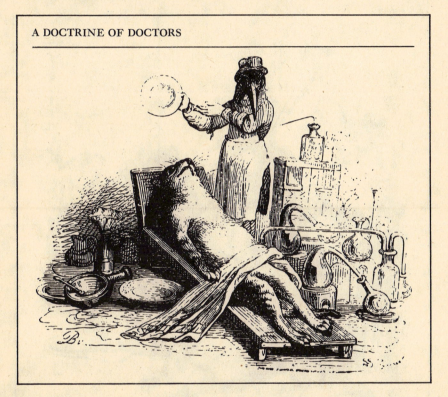

A SENTENCE OF JUDGES

Any doubt that these social terms had wide currency should be dispelled by the recollection that, in more recent times, a fast coach was still called "a diligence."

A STATE OF PRINCES

A HOST OF MEN
See the earlier note on HOST OF ANGELS
A ROUTE OF KNIGHTS
See the previous note on ROUTE OF WOLVES.
AN IMPATIENCE OF WIVES
A PRUDENCE OF VICARS
AN OBEISANCE OF SERVANTS
A SET OF USHERS

A DRAUGHT OF BOTTLERS

A TEMPERANCE OF COOKS

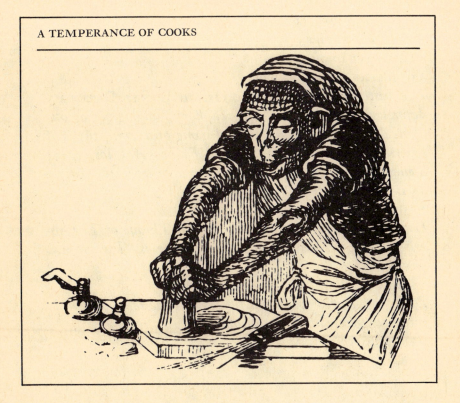

A STALK OF FORESTERS

A BOAST OF SOLDIERS

A LAUGHTER OF HOSTLERS

A CAJOLERY OF TAVERNERS

The vast and comprehensive Oxford English Dictionary *defines* glozing *as "flattering, cajolery," and gives as one of its definitions, "3. An alleged name of a 'company' (of taverners) 1486* Bk. St. Albans *Fvi b, A Glosyng of Tauerneris," which is how the term appears in the list.*

AN IMPERTINENCE OF PEDDLERS

A THRAVE OF THRESHERS

Under "thresher" the OED *quotes "A Thraue of Throsheris" from* St. Albans, *and defines* thrave *as "Two shocks of corn."*

A SQUAT OF DAUBERS

Daubers repaired walls and fences and the term obviously refers to their working position.

A FIGHTING OF BEGGARS

A MELODY OF HARPISTS
A POVERTY OF PIPERS

In the fifteenth century it was wiser, it seems, to take up the harp than the pipes.

A NEVERTHRIVING OF JUGGLERS

Obviously they had it no better than pipers.

A SUBTLETY OF SERGEANTS

This term confused me greatly: of the sergeants I have known, very few were subtle, and I couldn't believe human nature had changed that much in a mere five hundred years. And so I began a slow search through dusty library stacks for the secret behind a sotelty of sergeauntis. I found it at the end of a very long list of definitions in an exceptionally musty volume. "Sergeant," the book said, was "a title borne by a lawyer." Case dismissed.

A DRIFT OF FISHERMEN

A BLACKENING OF SHOEMAKERS

This one was thorny too. What Dame Juliana said was a Bleche of sowteris. *I found this singularly unilluminating, but another trek through the athenaeal dust revealed that* sowters *were shoemakers and that* bleche *meant either "bleach" or "blacken" (from the OE* blæcean). *I opted for "blacken." It may have been the dust.*

A SMIRK OF COURIERS

The original is a Smere of Coryouris. *To "laugh smere" is to laugh lightly, mockingly. "Smirk" is derived from it.*

A CLUSTER OF GRAPES

Yes, a genuine venereal term, codified 500 years ago.

A CLUSTER OF CHURLS

AN EXAMPLE OF MASTERS

In the note on rag of colts I indicated that we would re-
encounter the term in a different context. Here it is, meaning not "anger" but "wantonness," from the OF ragier.
A rather sad commentary on fifteenth-century maiden-
hood—or the want of it.

This splendid venereal term also inspired some interesting digging—that led to fascinating provenances. It appears in the list as an vncredibilitie of Cocoldis, which doesn't seem to make much sense: cuckolds have good reason to be incredulous, but no one doubts their existence, which

vncredibilitie *would seem to imply. I assumed that somehow, at some time, "incredibility" must have meant "in-
credulity" as well and so translated it. Then I began a
diffident search for some kind of confirmation. I was astonished to find that the OED, under* uncredible, *gave
the expected "incredible" as its first definition, but the
definitely* unexpected *"incredulous" as its second. I had
been instinctively right—and now I had proof. What was
my proof? The mighty, magisterial* Oxford English
Dictionary *says so. But even the OED must support its
views, and whom does Dr. Murray offer as* his *authority?
Dame Juliana! "Incredulous," says the OED, and points
for proof to "1486* Bk. of St. Albans *f vj b,* An vncredibilitie of Cocoldis." *The logic is suspiciously circular, and
it's a bit like being offered your own watch as collateral,
but I think I'm ready to settle.*

Here is another term we have encountered before. In an earlier note I suggested that you remember raff. *The moment has come to resurrect it. This term appears in the St. Albans list as a* Rafull of knauys. *The OED refers you from "rafull" or "rayful" to "raffle," and we are back to our root* raff, *obviously a very popular word in the fifteenth century. This time we are told that "raffle" had as one of its meanings* riffraff, *and we have our translation.*

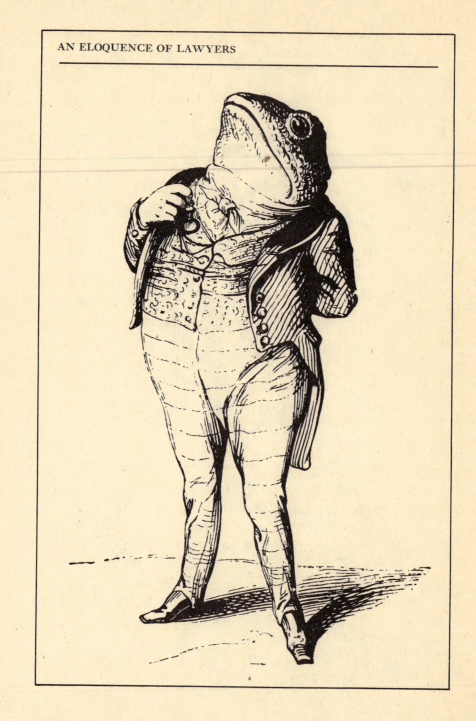

A SKULK OF THIEVES

A PONTIFICALITY OF PRELATES

AN OBSERVANCE OF HERMITS

AN EXECUTION OF OFFICERS

A FAITH OF MERCHANTS
Clearly meant sarcastically.

A SAFEGUARD OF PORTERS

A GAGGLE OF WOMEN

The key to this term also lay at the end of a rather tortuous, labyrinthian path, and, on the theory that the reader isn't too exhausted to make one more expedition with me back to the fifteenth century, I will retrace my steps. The Book of St. Albans *was printed just ten years after the date that is generally taken as the dividing line between Middle and Modern English, and, to the inexpert eye, some of these terms can appear impenetrable. Take this one: what would you make of* a Trynket of Corueseris? *Well, you would begin with* Corueseris. *The "is," you know, is a fifteenth-century plural form. And you take the "u" for a "v" because it makes sense euphonically. Now you have the singular "corveser," and this is where you begin in the OED, which says that "corveser" is a variant of "corviser." Very well, you move on to "corviser" and search through all the orthographic shapes it has taken through the centuries, coming finally to "corueseris, from F.* courvoisier, shoemaker." *We seem to have half our term, but why a* trynket? *Quickly enough you discover that the OED has "tryn" as a variant spelling of "trin," and then you come to the* coup de foudre. *Under "trinket" the OED says: "From the similarity of form, it has been suggested that this is the same word as Trenket, or* trynket, *a small knife, spec. a shoemaker's knife."* Eureka.

The term is Misbeleue *which, according to the OED, has more the sense of "erroneous belief" than "refusal to believe"; hence "illusion" in the sense of "trompe-l'œil." The OED also gives the term, in its original orthography, as a "term for a 'company' of painters."*

A LASH OF CARTERS

A DIGNITY OF CANONS

A CHARGE OF CURATES

A DISCRETION OF PRIESTS

A SKULK OF FRIARS

AN ABOMINABLE SIGHT OF MONKS

The Church was doing something wrong in England. If Pope Clement had read The Book of St. Albans *England might be Catholic today!*

A BLAST OF HUNTERS

A THREATENING OF COURTIERS

A PROMISE OF TAPSTERS

A LYING OF PARDONERS

A GORING OF BUTCHERS

A SCOLDING OF SEAMSTRESSES

A WANDERING OF TINKERS

A DRUNKENNESS OF COBBLERS

The term in St. Albans *is* Dronkship. *Says the OED: "Drunkship-DRUNKENNESS. b. a drunken company 1486* Bk. of St. Albans *F vij, a dronkship of Coblers."*

A CLUSTER OF KNOTS

A RASCAL OF BOYS

Vide *the earlier note on* rascal.

A DISWORSHIP OF SCOTS

Probably a reference to the reverence of writers for their patrons and not, alas, vice versa.

So you see, by 1486 the venereal game was already in full swing. There are examples of it in most of the early manuscripts. The first *Harley Manuscript* gives GAGGLE OF GOSSIPS, and the very early book *The Hors, Shepe, & the Ghoos* contributes A PITY OF PRISONERS and A HASTINESS OF COOKS. The extreme importance of these books in the fifteenth century is indicated by the fact that the last named was one of the first printed by William Caxton in the year that he introduced printing to England. And if we are still inclined to think of the social terms of venery as frivolous, C. E. Hare asserts that A BLAST OF HUNTERS and its fellows "were all probably in use at one time or another." There is of course no law or canon of usage that gives any of these terms sole possession of the field, but clearly they were once considered well enough established to take their places with A FLOCK OF SHEEP and A SCHOOL OF FISH.

        But, that the codifiers of these terms knew they were playing a word game is equally clear, from the terms themselves—and the history of the game in the centuries since Caxton. It has never stopped. The reader of this book may already know the popular philological story that usually takes Oxford as its locale. In it, four dons, each representing a different academic discipline and therefore a different viewpoint, were flapping along the Oxford High when their path was crossed by a small but conspicuous group of prostitutes. The quickest of the dons muttered, "A jam of tarts." The second, obviously a fellow in Music, riposted, "No, a flourish of strumpets." From the third, apparently an expert on nineteenth-century English literature, came, "Not at all . . . an essay of Trollope's." The fourth—Modern English Literature—said, "An anthology of pros." (I have heard versions that included "a peal of Jezebels," "a smelting of ores" and even "a troop of horse," but this begins to be flogging a dead one.)

Besides, the dons' venereal terms, as brilliantly constructed as they are, seem to me to obscure the point of the venereal game by drawing attention to both ends of the phrase; that is, not only to the term, "anthology," but its object, already a synonym, "pros." What we are admiring is verbal dexterity and ingenuity; what emerges is not poetry but a joke, not revelation but a chuckle.

There has, of course, through the long history of the game, always been the temptation to make a joke of it, and sometimes the temptation is irresistible. I began playing the venereal game long before I knew that Dame Juliana (or anyone else) had. For a few euphoric days I thought I had invented it. And I have often been tempted by the punning aspect of the game, as when I decided that a group of male homosexuals should be known as "a charm of fairies," "a basket of fruit," "a bundle of faggots" (in England, "a packet of fags"), "a board of trade," or "a burrow of Queens." Though I'm rather pleased with some of these terms as verbal machinery, I have ended by striking them *en masse* from the list that follows. For me they fail to qualify for the same reason as those of the illustrious dons.

Having taken this high-handed attitude toward what a venereal term is *not*, I suppose it is incumbent on me to try to explain as briefly and precisely as I can what I think it *is*. First of all, obviously, I think it is poetry. Robert Frost wrote, "There are many other things I have found myself saying about poetry, but the chiefest of these is that it is metaphor, saying one thing and meaning another, saying one thing in *terms* of another." (Italics mine.)

Certainly, by this definition the venereal terms are the essence of poetry, the "chiefest" thing, for they are unalloyed metaphor. More specifically, most of them are synechdochic in form, letting a quintessential part (PRIDE, LEAP, GAGGLE, SKULK) stand for the whole, giving us large illuminations in small flashes.

My principal objection to the dons' terms, and my "charm of fairies," etc., is that they do not say "one thing in terms of another"; they say *two* things, both "essay" and "Trollope's"; and, lost in admiration for the double *double entendre (quadruple entendre?)*, we lose poetry and illumination too. We have witnessed some verbal sleight-of-hand; but "anthology" and "jam" tell us nothing about whores, and that is, or *should* be, the purpose of the game. At least it is in the best examples I can think of, *e.g.*, A PARLIAMENT OF OWLS—"parliament" tells us something, it gives us a valuable quiddity of owls.

My position on this is, of course, much too dogmatic. A joke may illuminate, and you will find a number of them that I couldn't resist in the list that follows. The only reason I have emphasized this point is that one of the basic rules of the venereal game is that it is the *term* that matters. In AN EXALTATION OF LARKS, "exaltation" is the operative word. If "larks" had been turned into a synonym that made a *jeu de mots* of the whole phrase, I feel that more might have been lost than gained.

In some cases, as perhaps in "a flourish of strumpets," we seem to have both joke and revelation, but, for me, "an anthology of pros" stands somewhere outside the venereal game, the goal of which, I feel, is to tell us something quintessentially true about the term's object—something we failed to notice or took for granted until that moment. The term of venery is a searchlight that *illuminates* something for us, letting us see it with fresh insight, or as if for the first time.

If you join in the venereal game—and by now it must be nakedly apparent that this book is an invitation to—you will probably find that your first attempts are almost all alliterative (like GAGGLE OF GEESE).

My advice, for what it is worth, is to fight that impulse. If the proper, poetic, illuminating term happens to be alliterative with the group it is describing, well and good; but if it is not, nothing is lost, and there may be a clearer focus on the main thing: the term, with its gingery secret. In the venereal game, as in the arts, simplicity is the goal and distillation is the way. "Omission," Lytton Strachey wrote in 1912, "is the beginning of all art."

Since the venereal game has been going on for more than five hundred years, there have been a great number of players. C. E. Hare, in his *Language of Field Sports*, assembled a long list of contemporary venereal terms from various sources, and some of them deserve repetition: AN OBSTINACY OF BUFFALOES, A BASK OF CROCODILES, A TOWER OF GIRAFFES, A POMP OF PEKINGESE, A CONDESCENSION OF ACTORS, A DEBAUCHERY OF BACHELORS, AN ERUDITION OF EDITORS, AN UNEMPLOYMENT OF GRADUATES, AN UNHAPPINESS OF HUSBANDS, AN EXAGGERATION OF FISHERMEN and A WOBBLE OF BICYCLES.

In a recent issue of the *Bulletin* of the Mensa Society, a doctor in California cut through the whole medical profession, coming up with such contemporary venereal terms as A BRACE OF ORTHOPEDISTS, A JOINT OF OSTEOPATHS, A RASH OF DERMATOLOGISTS, A FLUTTER OF CARDIOLOGISTS, A GUESS OF DIAGNOSTICIANS, A PILE OF PROCTOLOGISTS, A CORPS OF ANATOMISTS and A SMEAR OF GYNECOLOGISTS.

The list that follows consists of the terms of venery that I have coined or encountered since I first began unearthing these shards of poetry and truth. I hasten to acknowledge that some of the terms are not mine. As I played the venereal game, like Tom Sawyer whitewashing his fence, I found that spectators didn't stay spectators long. If you should feel the urge, there are more brushes in the pail.

94   A TRANCE OF LOVERS
          A PIDDLE OF PUPPIES
          A TRIP OF HIPPIES

A SLOUCH OF MODELS

A FLUSH OF PLUMBERS

A WINCE OF DENTISTS

A LURCH OF BUSSES

AN ESCHEAT OF LAWYERS

A WRANGLE OF PHILOSOPHERS

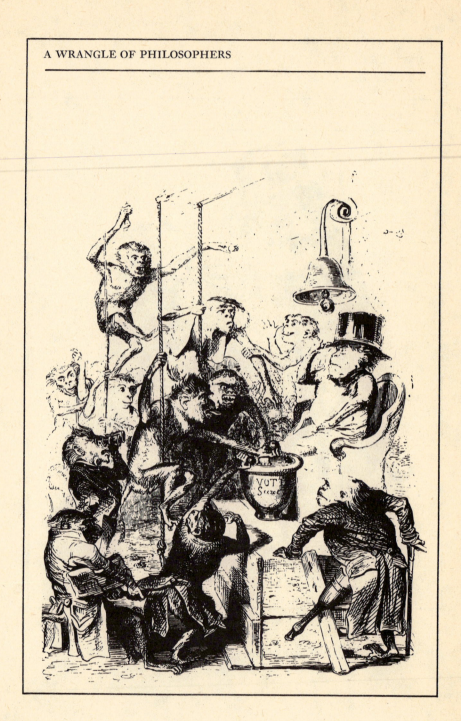

A SNEER OF BUTLERS

A DISAGREEMENT OF STATESMEN

A CRUNCH OF WRESTLERS

A STRING OF VIOLINISTS

A BABBLE OF BARBERS

AN ACNE OF ADOLESCENTS

A NERVE OF NEIGHBORS

A MERDE OF CANICHES

A POUND OF PIANISTS

A SHOWER OF METEOROLOGISTS

AN INDIFFERENCE OF WAITERS

A BLOAT OF HIPPOPOTAMI

A SWISH OF HAIRDRESSERS

AN INTRUSION OF COCKROACHES

A SAMPLE OF SALESMEN

A FUMBLE OF CHECKGRABBERS

A FROST OF DOWAGERS

A WHINE OF CLARINETISTS

A CONJUNCTION OF GRAMMARIANS

A LEER OF BOYS

A GIGGLE OF GIRLS

A FLAP OF NUNS

A DASH OF COMMUTERS

A STUD OF POKER PLAYERS

A MUTTER OF MOTHERS-IN-LAW

A MASS OF PRIESTS

A MADDER OF PAINTERS

A PURÉE OF STRAPHANGERS

A GOGGLE OF AVIATORS

A DELIRIUM OF DEBUTANTES

A PRANCE OF EQUESTRIANS

AN AROMA OF BAKERS

A CAPER OF KIDS

A TRINE OF ASTROLOGERS

A BELLYFUL OF BORES

A SLAVER OF GLUTTONS

A SAUNTER OF COWBOYS

A PRATFALL OF CLOWNS

A NUCLEUS OF PHYSICISTS

A PUMMEL OF MASSEURS

A RING OF JEWELERS

AN UNCTION OF UNDERTAKERS

An even larger group:
AN EXTREME UNCTION OF UNDERTAKERS

A FLOAT OF DANCERS (*female*)

A FLIGHT OF DANCERS (*male*)

A SHRIVEL OF CRITICS

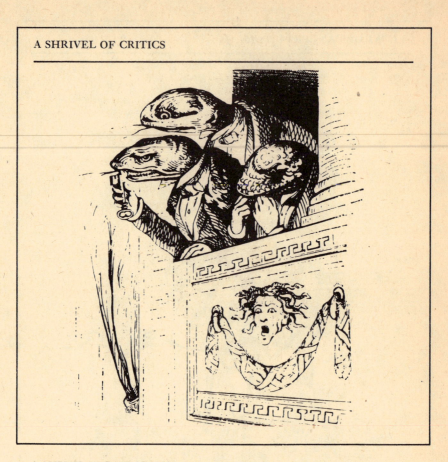

A SHUSH OF LIBRARIANS

A HACK OF SMOKERS

A DÉLICATESSE OF GOURMETS

A DELICATESSEN OF GOURMANDS

AN OHM OF ELECTRICIANS

A BLUR OF IMPRESSIONISTS

A GULP OF CORMORANTS

A STAND OF FLAMINGOES

A FAMILY OF BIOLOGISTS

A PROFIT OF GURUS

AN OGLE OF OFFICE BOYS

A STORE OF GYPSIES

A COLLOID OF CHEMISTS

A LOAD OF DRUNKS

In England: A STONE OF DRUNKS

A HAGGLE OF VENDORS

A CURSE OF CREDITORS

A SLUMBER OF OLD GUARD

A PORTFOLIO OF BROKERS

A SKIRL OF PIPERS

A WIGGLE OF STARLETS

A PINCH OF PRODUCERS

A STRANGLE OF CITY-DWELLERS

A TABULA RASA OF EMPIRICISTS

A MEWS OF CATHOUSES

A SPRINKLING OF GARDENERS

A CONCATENATION OF ORGIASTS

A PARLAY OF HORSEPLAYERS

A CLICK OF PHOTOGRAPHERS

A NO-NO OF NANNIES

A SCORE OF BACHELORS

A PALLOR OF NIGHTWATCHMEN

A BUZZ OF BARFLIES

A CONSTERNATION OF MOTHERS

A THRILL OF FANS

A GRAFT OF TREE SURGEONS

A SLANT OF JOURNALISTS

A CHARGE OF TAXIS

A SCHREI OF HELDENTENOREN

A RUMBLE OF BASSES   A QUAVER OF COLORATURAS

A SHRIEK OF CLAQUES

A RECESSION OF ECONOMISTS

A PAVANNE OF MATADORS

A LEAP OF BANDERILLEROS

A COMPLEX OF PSYCHOANALYSTS

A BROOD OF CHESSPLAYERS

A TORQUE OF MECHANICS

A HORDE OF MISERS

AN ENTRANCE OF ACTRESSES

AN AMBUSH OF WIDOWS

A MESS OF OFFICERS

A PARENTHESIS OF CELLISTS

A PERSISTENCE OF PARENTS

AN INGRATITUDE OF CHILDREN

A FAILING OF STUDENTS

A DILATION OF PUPILS *(after Dr. Leary)*

A TRANSPLANT OF SUBURBANITES

A CONGLOMERATE OF GEOLOGISTS

A BLARNEY OF BARTENDERS

This is simply a contemporary translation of St. Alban's
A Glosyng of Tauerneris, q.v. *in the introduction to this
section, in the note to* A CAJOLERY OF TAVERNERS.

A DROVE OF CABDRIVERS

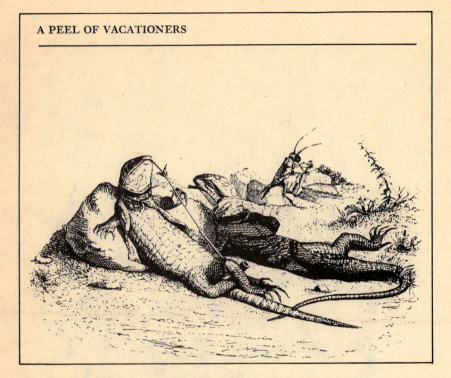

AN EXPLOSION OF ITALIANS
A GROSS OF GERMANS
A PECK OF FRENCHMEN
A POUND OF ENGLISHMEN
A PINT OF IRISHMEN
A FIFTH OF SCOTS
AN INVASION OF ISRAELIS
A FLIGHT OF ARABS
A WATCH OF SWISS

A DESCENT OF RELATIVES

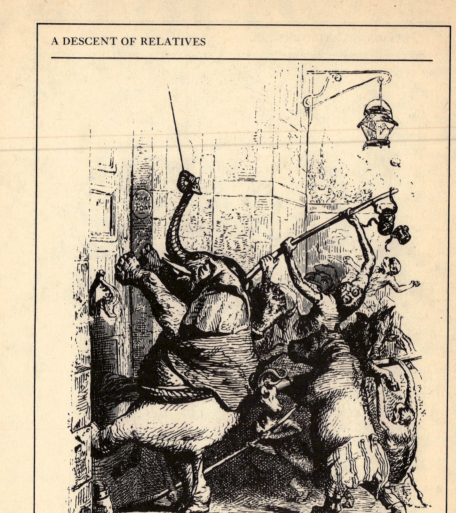

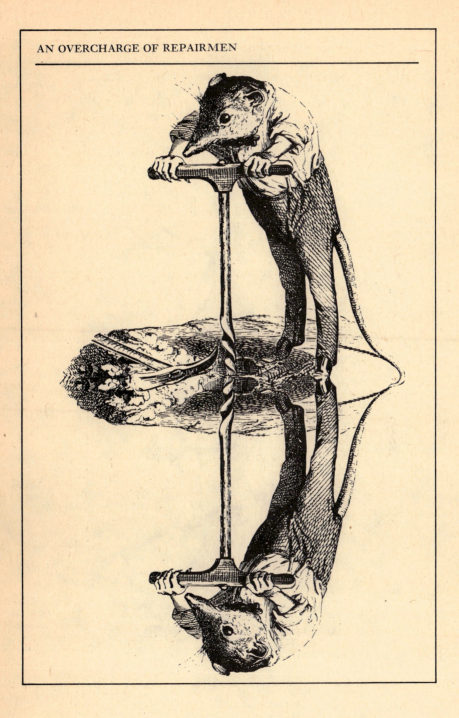

PART IV

THE SERENDIPITOUS

Having read this far, you know that
the introduction to Part III of this book ended with an
invitation to its readers to take brushes from the pail and
begin adding their own venereal graffiti to the fence. When
I made that offer I had no inkling that so many hands
would reach for the pail. In the nine years since the publication of *An Exaltation of Larks* a wild-eyed philological
underground, every bit as passionate in its pursuit of words
as the sixteenth-century neologists who evoked my wistful
admiration in the introduction to Part I, has emerged from
the cracks, crannies, fissures, caves and assorted other
secret places to which an antilexic world had driven them.

From every corner of the globe I have
received letters bearing everything from a single treasured
invention to a logorrheic flood. Textbooks have challenged
students to join the venereal game, and the students' re-
sponses have brought fresh bursts of inspiration to my
doorstep. Contributors to periodicals of every sort have
used this book like sourdough, to leaven new batches of
terms; and radio and television programs have entered the
lists, literally and figuratively.

In sum, I have been the happy recipient
of A TIDAL WAVE OF TERMS, which I am pleased to pass
along to you—to leaven the next batch. Some of the terms
that follow are of my devising; some were transmitted
across dinner tables, confided in theater lobbies, or thrust
at me on the street; and others materialized in my mailbox,
through the caring camaraderie of the defenders of the
philological faith unearthed—and unleashed—by the publication of this book.

When I wrote *An Exaltation of Larks*
I was unable to dispel the pale cast of pessimism that sick-
lied o'er several paragraphs in the introduction to Part I

(and clings like a particularly tenacious fog to pages 15 and 16 of this edition). In point of fact I held out so little hope for the future of the written word that I thought of my precious hoard of venereal terms as a kind of linguistic rear guard, digging in for an almost certainly last-ditch stand against the massed battalions of the anti-verbal army looming smug and ominous in every direction.

But I am delighted—and astonished—to report that the distant sound of a fusty bugle hinted at rescue, and over the horizon an antic, antique troop of cavalry appeared, trailing its outdated and overmatched caissons of words. Mild metaphor was pitted against gleaming tubes and diodes, gentle irony and subtle anastrophe confronted the awesome power of Trinitron and Sensurround, as the defenders of the word gallantly flung their outmoded resources at the sleek electronic hardware ranged against them. The point is still at issue, but the next pages are heartening evidence that the embattled word doesn't stand alone and undefended, as I feared when I ventured timidly onto the battlefield almost a decade ago.

Space doesn't permit acknowledgment of every warrior on the field (and in the case of many of the terms on the following pages accreditation would be impossible since they were the product of several minds arriving discretely at the same inspiration). But to the creators of all these collectives—collectively—a deep, and deeply grateful, bow.

122   A QUIRE OF ANGELS
       A LITER OF CHEMISTS
       A METER OF PERCUSSIONISTS
       A CC OF MEXICANS
       A POUND OF CARPENTERS

A SHILLING OF BARKERS

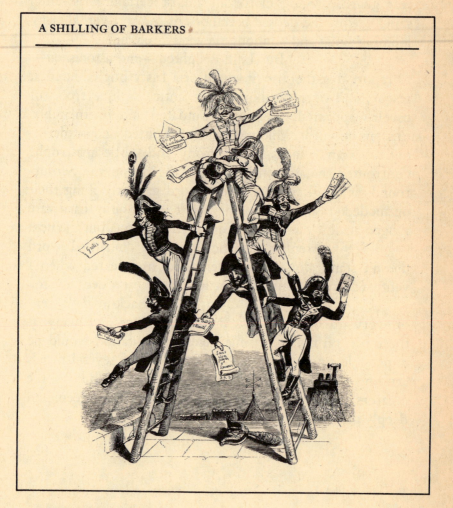

A VIAL OF BORGIAS
A NUMBER OF STATISTICIANS
A LOT OF USED CAR DEALERS

A DISH OF GOSSIPS

A POT OF DIETERS
A PAN OF REVIEWERS
A SCOOP OF REPORTERS
A MAGNUM OF HIT MEN
in pursuit of
A SPLIT OF DEBTORS

124   A STRIP OF ECDYSIASTS
A GRIP OF PORTERS
A SCREAM OF NEWSBOYS
James Joyce in Ulysses.
A BOUQUET OF WINETASTERS
A SLEW OF EXTERMINATORS
A BORED OF TRUSTEES
A STAMPEDE OF PHILATELISTS
A TRUCULENCE OF MOVING MEN
A FLUSH OF W.C.'S
RAF collective for Wing Commanders.

A PHALANX OF FLASHERS

A RIOT OF COMEDIANS
A SPATE OF INGENUES
A SPITE OF PRIMA DONNAS
A SET OF DESIGNERS
AN ASSEMBLÉE OF CHOREOGRAPHERS

A BRACE OF STAGEHANDS

A MEASURE OF WARDROBE LADIES

A GILD OF DIRECTORS

A PANIC OF PRODUCERS

A PLOT OF PLAYWRIGHTS

A GLAZE OF TOURISTS

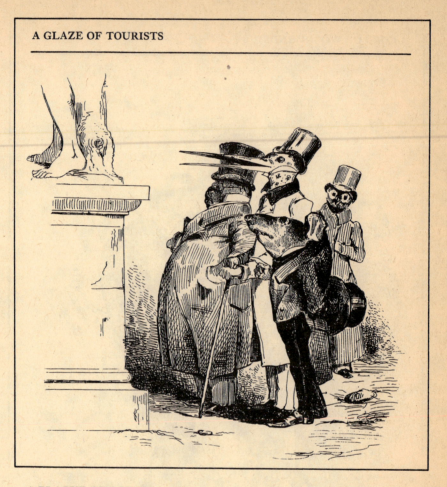

A PLAGUE OF LOCALS
AN EXPECTATION OF HEIRS
A GUSH OF SYCOPHANTS
A ROOD OF BOORS
A BED OF SWINGERS
A GROPE OF GROUPIES
A SHRIEK OF CONTESTANTS

A TRAVESTY OF TRANSVESTITES

A PLENITUDE OF FRESHMEN

A PLATITUDE OF SOPHOMORES

A GRATITUDE OF JUNIORS

AN ATTITUDE OF SENIORS

A FORTITUDE OF GRADUATE STUDENTS

AN AVUNCULUS OF ALUMNI

A CLAMBER OF ASSISTANT PROFESSORS

A TENURE OF ASSOCIATE PROFESSORS

AN ENTRENCHMENT OF FULL PROFESSORS

AN EX CATHEDRA OF PROFESSORS EMERITI

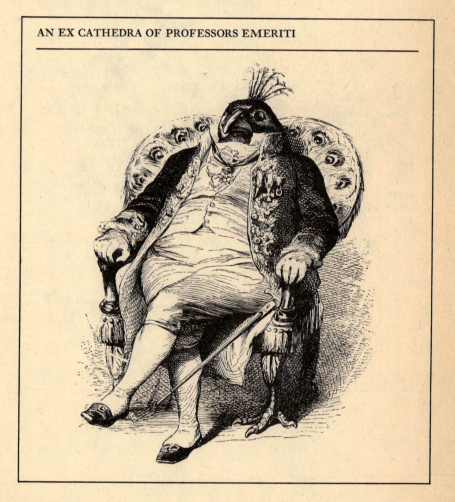

A DROWSE OF UNDERACHIEVERS
A LEAP OF OVERACHIEVERS
A PALLOR OF NIGHT STUDENTS

A DRIFT OF LECTURERS

A BROOD OF RESEARCHERS
A DISCORD OF EXPERTS

A HIVE OF ALLERGISTS

A VOID OF UROLOGISTS

A SERIES OF RADIOLOGISTS

A COLONY OF BACTERIOLOGISTS

A HOST OF EPIDEMIOLOGISTS

A HELIX OF GENETICISTS

A WHEEZE OF JOGGERS
A ROW OF OARSMEN
A LIE OF GOLFERS
A BOWL OF KEGLERS
Or vice versa.
A TUMBLER OF GYMNASTS
A RACE OF JOCKEYS

A SHIVER OF SHARKS
A SCURRY OF SQUIRRELS
A GLINT OF GOLDFISH
A POUNCE OF CATS
A SCOLD OF JAYS
A CHAIN OF BOBOLINKS
A WAKE OF BUZZARDS
A RUN OF COYOTES
A ROMP OF OTTERS
A GAZE OF RACCOONS
AN IMPLAUSIBILITY OF GNUS
A KETTLE OF FISH

A FINE KETTLE OF FISH
In the better neighborhoods.

For a term of relatively recent vintage, this expression has achieved wide usage in recent years, and is almost universally applicable today in such expressions as, "The company will shortly issue its latest breakdown of plans."
In the same vein:

A COMEDY OF AIRLINE SCHEDULES

A TRAGEDY OF RAILROAD SCHEDULES

A HOVER OF HELICOPTERS

A STACK OF PLANES

A POSTPONEMENT OF TRAINS

A CANCELLATION OF TRAINS
On suburban lines.

AN EMBARRASSMENT OF TWITCHES

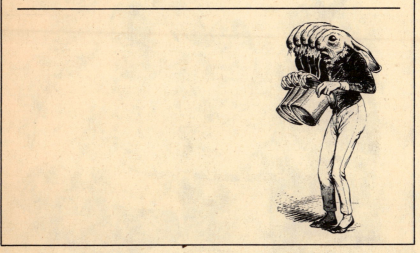

A BREACH OF PREMISES
Law-enforcement terminology for a case of breaking and entering by a former husband, wife, or lover.

A QUINCUNX OF PLANETS
A proper term for any group of five objects placed in a square, with four of the objects at the square's corners and one at its center.

A GLUT OF COMMERCIALS

A RHAPSODY OF BLUES

A HO HO! OF LOOPHOLES

AN OH OH! OF AUDITS

A PITFALL OF FINE PRINT

AN OBSOLESCENCE OF APPLIANCES

A METAMORPHOSIS OF OVOIDS

Said of hatching eggs, esp. in 1st-century Rome.

A CLUTCH OF SECOND THOUGHTS
A FLIGHT OF YESTERDAYS
A TWINKLING OF TODAYS

A PROMISE OF TOMORROWS

The language lives.
The venereal game continues.
Your move.

Explicit
James Lipton
in
An Exaltation of Larks

A pride of lions.
A shrewdness of apes.
A parliament of owls.
An exaltation of larks.
All are terms of venery, those imaginative collective
nouns that evolved in the Middle Ages when the sophis-
ticated art of hunting demanded an equally sophis-
ticated vocabulary. In addition to a passion for sport,
our forebears also delighted in the play of words, and
so the use of such fanciful phrases became codified,
naming particular groups of humans as well as all
manner of other creatures. James Lipton has taken
the next logical step and invented many new terms of
venery as well, to fit the modern world: *a wince
of dentists, a pound of carpenters, a lot of used car
dealers.* And so the venereal game goes on.

Both the wit and the poetry of these language
treasures, old and new, are enhanced by curiously appro-
priate illustrations from the work of such masters as
Dürer and Grandville.

"A charming book for any occasion . . . literary, tasteful,
ingenious, and good fun"   —John Barkham

"Will be gobbled up by anyone who enjoys words and
wordplay . . . a truly handsome volume"   —*Book World*

"Joyous and informative reading . . . a perfect gift for
anyone with an I.Q. worth noting."   —*Saturday Review*

AUST. $8.95
(recommended)
CAN. $9.95
U.S.A. $7.95

Language

ISBN 0 14
00.4536 8